Bringing the London 2012 Games to the Lea Valley

East London has a proud history, but the area where the Olympic Park has been built was often seen as either flood-prone marsh or a contaminated industrial site. In fact we have inherited a site left by a strong and resilient working community who played an important role not only in the history of London, but more widely in Britain and the world.

The name of the River Lea, believed to come from a Celtic word – *lug* – meaning 'bright', may be a clue as to why prehistoric farmers came to settle on its banks. Later, the floodplain provided rich grazing

In time, the valley became London's workshop, providing room for its reservoirs and railway yards, land for its essential industries, and playing a vital, if unheralded, role in the nation's wartime defence. Now it starts a new life – as the venue for the London 2012 Olympic and Paralympic Games, and afterwards, as a new quarter of east London, with the Queen Elizabeth Olympic Park the focus for the new sporting venues, housing and parklands.

The Olympic Stadium at the centre of the Olympic Park

A finds specialist examining clay tobacco pipes

The investigations

In 2005, as soon as London won its bid to host the 2012 Games, a programme of archaeological and historical research into the cultural heritage of the Olympic Park site was set in motion. Specialists in a wide range of disciplines examined all aspects of the area's past.

That past started with the end of the last Ice Age, when water from melting glaciers first surged down the valley into the Thames. The investigations continued right up to the present, with the recording of people's memories of growing up in the area, wartime life, and work in local factories.

The investigations have revealed the extraordinary diversity of ordinary lives lived in this changing landscape. They have shown how people sometimes conserved and, at other times, rapidly changed their surroundings and how, in turn, their lives were shaped by wider influences – environmental changes, technological developments, economic forces and political events.

These changes continue today, as the area is again transformed by a global event – the 2012 Games.

Revealing a timber of a Roman river structure

Methods of investigation

Documentary research

Much has been learnt about the site's past by examining historical records, old maps and drawings. These helped to indicate where on the site archaeologists should excavate, and which buildings and structures they should record.

They also provide invaluable historical detail about places and people, and about their economic and social lives. They show how the landscape and the streetscape, even individual buildings, have changed over time.

Geoarchaeology

The data from almost 4,000 geotechnical boreholes drilled across and around the site were analysed, revealing the deep layers of natural and modern dumped deposits. From these it was possible to reconstruct the topography of the buried landscape first occupied in early prehistory. Finding the courses of the ancient river channels has helped to explain the patterns of early settlement and farming.

More recent deposits, from the 19th and 20th centuries, are associated with the development of industry, and modern landfill of wartime demolition rubble, and waste disposal.

Left: One of the valley's windmills, Stent's Mill, blown down in 1834

Right: Borehole drilling rig collecting geoarchaeology sample

Archaeology

Before construction of the Olympic Park began, 121 evaluation trenches were excavated across the site. Many of them had deep, stepped sides, as the overlying deposits had to be removed by machine to allow the safe examination of the archaeological layers below.

The trenches exposed numerous archaeological features – including ditches, houses, pits, post-holes, and timber structures – of many different dates. These were excavated and recorded, with finds recovered from them and environmental samples taken.

A deep, stepped evaluation trench

Discoveries in eight of the trenches led to a second stage of archaeological work – detailed excavations. These revealed sites of Neolithic riverside activity, Bronze Age and Iron Age farming and settlement, a medieval millstream, a river boat abandoned beside a 19th-century windmill, and a Victorian industrial estate with its workers' cottages.

Iron Age round-house on the site of the Aquatics Centre

Reconstruction of the 19th-century windmill and boat at Nobshill Mill

Finds analysis

Over 10,000 archaeological objects were recovered during the investigations – coincidentally spanning more than 10,000 years. Each piece was carefully lifted and recorded, then cleaned, compared and analysed, and in some cases drawn.

Some types of finds, such as different forms of prehistoric pottery, helped us determine the dates of sites. The waterlogged ground in many trenches meant that some materials that do not usually survive, such as objects of wood and leather, were well preserved.

The earliest finds were objects made from flint, including a finely shaped Neolithic axe head. Prehistoric pottery, fired clay loom-weights, animal bones, pieces of worked wood and human skeletal remains were also found.

From more recent times, there were objects of bone, ivory, glass, ceramics, metal, stone, leather and wood. Some of the objects had been made locally, while others were mass produced elsewhere.

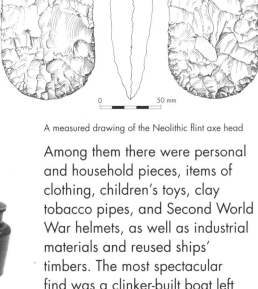

A measured drawing of the Neolithic flint axe head

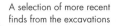

A selection of more recent finds from the excavations

Among them there were personal and household pieces, items of clothing, children's toys, clay tobacco pipes, and Second World War helmets, as well as industrial materials and reused ships' timbers. The most spectacular find was a clinker-built boat left abandoned in a river channel.

Environmental analysis

To understand how past environments affected where people lived and worked, and how people changed their surroundings, hundreds of soil samples were collected. These were taken from archaeological features, such as pits, hearths, and ditches, and from the natural sediments that slowly accumulated on the valley floor.

The samples contained the remains of plants (seeds, charcoal and pollen) and animals (bones, insects, snails and microscopic creatures), preserved either in the waterlogged ground conditions or by being charred by fire.

Different processes were used to extract the often microscopic remains from the soil samples, and some of the remains provided material for radiocarbon dating.

The identification and laboratory analysis of the extracted remains have allowed the environmental specialists to tell the story of the valley's changing environment, its soils and vegetation. They have revealed important information about how the land was exploited and the river managed, about farming and other economic activities, and about people's diet.

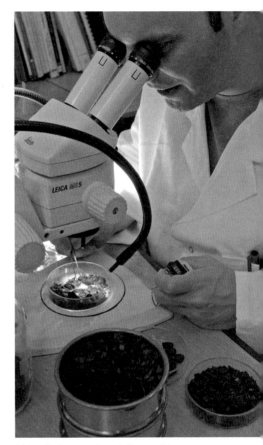

Above: Environmental specialist examining charred plant remains

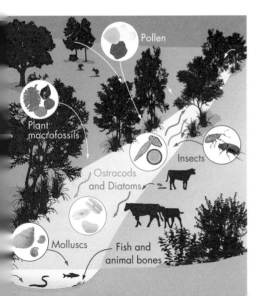

Left: Forms of environmental evidence

7

Building recording

Not all the important remains within the Olympic Park site were deeply buried. In order to create a record of the site's built heritage, 52 individual or groups of buildings and other structures were examined, and recorded.

Some of these were industrial premises, such as the Clarnico confectionery works at Kings Yard in Hackney Wick, and Yardley's soap and perfume factory on Carpenter's Road.

Elevation drawing of the Yardley & Co soap and perfume factory on Carpenter's Road

Early 20th-century footbridge across City Mill River

Others were associated with the complex of waterways that flow through the Park, such as Old Ford Lock at the southern end of the Hackney Cut, the tipping wharfs next to Gliksten's timber yard, or the wooden revetment supporting the riverbank on Potter's Ditch.

Others relate to the extensive infrastructure of railways, roads, bridges and reservoirs that transformed the appearance of the landscape in the first half of the 19th century, or to the defence structures from the Second World War.

Community engagement

Involving and informing the local community was a priority from the start of the investigations. The ODA's Discover programme shared the early results with children, students and teachers, as well as local residents and interest groups. There were workshops, and talks and displays, where people could handle for themselves some of the objects found.

Later, there was a Community History Programme based at, and using the resources of, Newham Heritage & Archives. This involved map and document workshops, which gave local people the opportunity to contribute their own knowledge of the area, and to participate in analysing the industrial development of Stratford using historical documents and old maps.

Another important element was the Oral History Project. This captured personal recollections of the area's recent past, of the social life, of work in its industries, and of growing up during wartime.

Open House event,
September 2010

The environmental and geoarchaeological evidence has revealed the valley's tundra landscape at the end of the last Ice Age, before the warmer climate attracted people back to Britain. From then, based on the evidence found, the story of the site can be divided into five broad epochs, each one distinct in the ways that communities occupied and exploited their surroundings.

The passage of time

Epoch 1
Hunter-gatherers and early settlers

The earliest finds were flints used by Mesolithic people who gathered plants, and hunted and fished as they moved through the valley. The woodland, marsh and river were exploited for their diverse resources even after people first adopted agriculture during the Neolithic period. These farmers used flint axes to cut down trees so they could cultivate crops, as well as to shape the wooden posts that were found driven into the river's edge, possibly for a trackway.

Epoch 2
Prehistoric farming communities

The earliest farmers left few traces in the valley, although the environmental evidence suggests their animals grazed on the marshy grassland. It was only later, in the Bronze Age and Iron Age, when people settled along the river banks, building round-houses, laying out rectangular fields, constructing ditched enclosures, and burying their dead, that we get an idea of how they organised their domestic and farming lives.

Schematic timeline
(based on finds from the Olympic Park)

12,000 – 10,000 BC
Late Glacial

8500 – 2200 BC
Mesolithic/Neolithic

2200 BC – AD 43
Bronze Age/Iron Age

Epoch 3
Developing London's hinterland

The Romans arrived in Britain in AD 43 and made their capital – *Londinium* – just to the west of the valley. They built a road through the site from *Camulodunum* (Colchester), although no trace of it was found. Both river and road would have been important for moving people and produce to the capital. After the Romans left, new peoples came – Saxons, Danes and in 1066 the Normans, but rural life probably changed little over this 1,000-year period.

Epoch 4
Mills and industry

The valley's economy was stimulated by the medieval monasteries and mills. The Knights Templar gave their name to the mills they owned at Temple Mills in the north of the Olympic Park. Such mills originally ground corn, but in the post-medieval period they manufactured many other goods as well. Only when Victorian railways and reservoirs transformed the valley, and new industries were powered by coal, oil and electricity, were the old mills superseded.

Epoch 5
20th century to third millennium

By 1900, London had spread far east of the River Lea. As a powerhouse of industry, the valley was a target during the Second World War and its defences were vital in resisting the bombing raids. Industry never fully recovered from the damage and large areas of the site were used for dumping demolition rubble, and later for waste landfill. However, 2005 – the year London won the bid for the 2012 Games – marked the start of a new epoch for the valley.

AD 43 – 1066
Roman/Saxon

AD 1066 – 1800
Medieval/post-medieval

20th century
Modern

An ancient riverbank

Probably the most complex archaeological deposits encountered during the investigations were recorded in Trench 118, just south of Stratford High Street, in the area of the Greenway Transport Hub. In this deep trench with stepped sides, channel sediments and riverside deposits were recorded going back around 13,000 years. As the river had repeatedly shifted its course, it had cut new channels through earlier sediments, sometimes moving archaeological remains from their original locations.

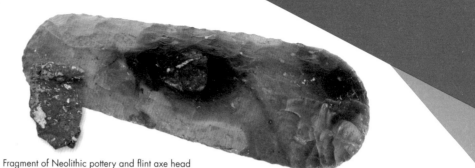

Fragment of Neolithic pottery and flint axe head

However, careful analysis of the resulting layers, and numerous radiocarbon dates obtained from archaeological and environmental remains, allowed the archaeologists to unravel the trench's complex stratigraphy, and identify channels dating to the Late Glacial, Neolithic, Bronze Age, and Roman periods. A medieval channel probably marks the early line of Waterworks River, before the Stratford causeway blocked its course in the 12th century.

The most significant finds dated to the Early Neolithic, the period when farming began in Britain. They included the only pieces of Neolithic pottery found in the whole of the Olympic Park investigations and a very finely made flint axe head. How the axe came to be left at this riverside location remains a mystery – perhaps it was a votive offering. But the spot was also marked by the rare survival of some form of Neolithic timber structure, possibly a riverside platform or trackway, represented by sharpened alder posts driven into the riverbank.

Exposing ancient channel deposits in Trench 118

Reconstruction of the Neolithic riverbank

Prehistoric settlement

Evidence of a prehistoric farmstead was found on the site of the Aquatics Centre. In Trench 24, a curving gully marked the edge of a Middle Bronze Age round-house. It was radiocarbon dated to around 1400 BC and is the earliest building known in the Olympic Park site. Just north of the house, in Trench 9, ditches had been dug to mark out large rectangular fields on the edge of a river channel. Finds from the ditch included pottery, flint, along with cattle and sheep bones, and charred grains from their crops.

People continued to live at this riverside location over many centuries. Late Bronze Age finds from large groups of pits included clay loom-weights used in weaving textiles. Some of the community's

Right: The prehistoric farming and settlement site

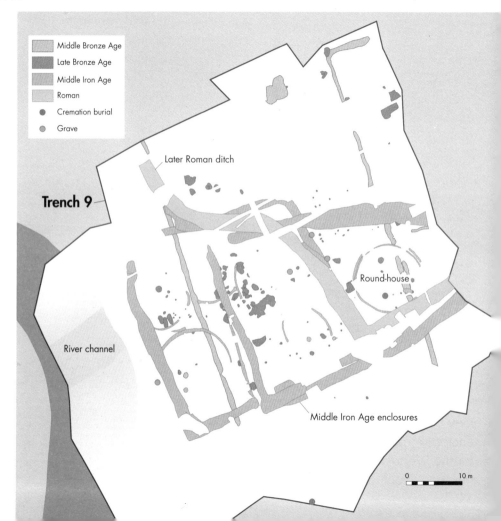

Middle Bronze Age
Late Bronze Age
Middle Iron Age
Roman
Cremation burial
Grave

Later Roman ditch

Trench 9

Round-house

River channel

Middle Iron Age enclosures

0   10 m

dead were buried on the site, their bodies having first been cremated; these were dated to around 1000 BC.

Around 300 BC, in the Middle Iron Age, there was a small cluster of round-houses at the same location. Seven houses were identified, although not all would have stood at the same time. One of the houses appears to have been rebuilt on the same spot. Just inside its doorway, a young goat had been buried in a pit – possibly some form of ritual offering.

As time passed, however, the river became more prone to flooding, and people moved to drier ground on the valley side. In their place they built a square ditched enclosure, possibly as a corral for the livestock they grazed on the valley floor. By the end of the Iron Age, the site appears to have been abandoned, although burials (of adults, male and female), no longer cremated, were still made there, suggesting that this was a long-term burial ground.

The land continued to be used in the Roman period, however, when a wide ditch was dug, winding around the edge of the Iron Age enclosure.

Above: Reconstruction of Bronze Age pottery (three on left) and Iron Age pottery (four on right)

Below: Excavating one of the burials on the site of the Aquatics Centre

15

Upstream of the Pudding Mills

Mills – watermills and windmills – were the backbone of industry from the medieval period to the Victorian era. Pudding Mill River, which branched off the River Lea just west of where the Olympic Stadium now stands, was one of the valley's mill-streams, powering a watermill to the south at Stratford. The mill was originally known as Fotes Mill (and later as St. Thomas's Mill, then Hart's Mill and finally as Pudding Mills).

Excavation in Trench 58, near the head of the river, revealed what may have been the course of an earlier stream for the mill. Its channel had been cleaned out a number of times, and on one occasion wattle revetments – willow rods woven around oak stakes – had been placed along the edges of the stream. These were preserved in the waterlogged conditions, and radiocarbon dated to around the 16th century.

Left: 1777 Chapman & André map, showing the millstreams, watermills and windmills in the Olympic Park area
Below: Wattle revetment in Trench 58

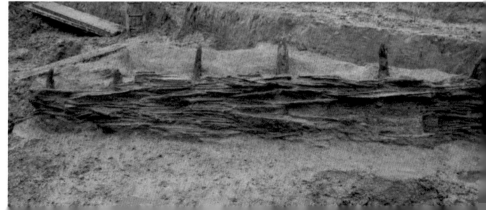

By the 19th century the stream had been abandoned and it was Pudding Mill River, excavated in Trench 59, which now powered the Pudding Mills. In 1807, a windmill was dismantled from its location on City Mill River and re-erected near the head of Pudding Mill River; maps show it was called 'Nobshill Mill (Corn)'. Next to the mill a more solid timber revetment was built along the river edge, which probably acted as a wharf for loading and unloading at the adjacent mill buildings.

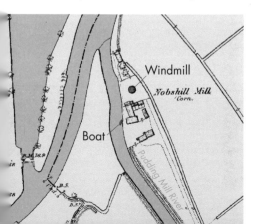

A small, clinker-built boat, well preserved in the river silts, was found lying against the wharf. It may have been built originally as a ship's tender for a larger, sea-going vessel, used for ferrying people to and from shore. Later a keel was added and it was converted to a small sailing boat, possibly a pleasure craft.

Finally, it was used as a gun punt, fitted with a large-barrelled shotgun, for wild-fowling on the waters of the lower River Lea and the Thames. Patched up and repaired over its long life, late in the 19th century it was eventually abandoned, possibly by the mill owner – just as the mill was.

Far left: 1868 map showing Nobshill Mill

Left: Excavating the boat

Below: Reconstruction of the Nobshill Mill boat fitted with a punt gun

Temple Mills industrial site

An excavation near the Velodrome, close to the site of the medieval watermills known as Temple Mills, uncovered important remains of the Olympic Park's industrial heritage, buried below 9m of modern landfill.

The site of the medieval mills, named after the Knights Templar who once owned them, lay outside the area of excavation. However, a water channel dating from at least as early as around 1500 was excavated. In later centuries,

Right: 19th-century features

Below: Recording the timber revetment on Tumbling Bay Stream

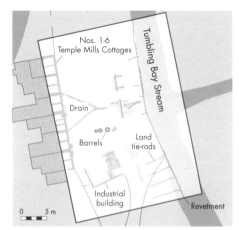

this channel became known as Tumbling Bay Stream (a 'tumbling bay' is an old term for a weir). It branched off the millstream at a weir above the mills and passed round their eastern side.

In the late 19th century, Tumbling Bay Stream had a solid timber revetment along its western bank, held in place by long iron tie-rods, connected to timber anchor plates buried in the ground.

As well as their medieval history, the Temple Mills are known from historical records to have been a site of industrial activity through the post-medieval period. One industrial building that was excavated had a furnace in one corner. This contained fragments of copper alloy slag, suggesting that it might have been part of a foundry owned by a company established in the 1690s to manufacture brass kettles.

Running along the south side of the building was a narrow water channel, lined with timbers reused from an earlier demolished building. The channel ran off Tumbling Bay Stream, and it was probably the wheel-pit for a water wheel, either powering bellows, or operating machinery in the foundry.

When the foundry was demolished a new building replaced it. Around the same time, c.1800, a terrace of six cottages was built on this small industrial estate. Only the fronts of the cottages, and their doorsteps, lay within the excavation, but the finds, such as crockery, glass, clay tobacco pipes, and metal objects, give an indication of their occupants' standard of living.

We can also see changes to the cottages during the 19th century, as lead pipes for water or gas were fed into the houses, and a new kerbed pavement was laid down in front. At the start of the 20th century, a cobbled road was built past the houses leading to new industrial premises to the south. The ruined shells of the cottages were still standing at the end of the Second World War.

Recording the Temple Mills cottages

Infrastructure for London and the Lea Valley

It was not industry that transformed the rural landscape of the Olympic Park site, but infrastructure. Firstly there were new navigation canals, with locks and floodgates along the waterways. Then with the coming of the railway, new embankments, bridges, viaducts, goods yards and depots were built, and as industry spread onto the valley floor, the road network was extended.

During the investigations some of the features of the valley's infrastructure relating to the supply of water and disposal of sewage were recorded.

Reservoirs

In 1809, the newly formed East London Waterworks Company started supplying drinking water from new works at Old Ford, where water from the River Lea was pumped into two brick-lined reservoirs. By 1830, two larger reservoirs had also been built on the opposite side of the river, supplied by a channel starting further upriver. However, the water in them was blamed for a series of cholera epidemics in the 1850s, and eventually they were closed down and filled in.

Also investigated was the wide entrance and discharge gate of a

Above: Substantial brick pier at the reservoir gate

Left: The compensation reservoir that stored tidal water for use by the watermills

'compensation reservoir', not for drinking water, in the west of the Park. This was filled up on the incoming tide, with the water being released through the gate when the tide ebbed and water levels in the river dropped. Its purpose was to compensate for the 5,900,000 gallons that the Waterworks Company were drawing off the river every day, which was affecting the operation of the watermills, and making navigation of the river more difficult.

Northern Outfall Sewer

As London expanded, problems with the city's sewers reached a crisis in 1858. Soaring summer temperatures resulted in the 'Great Stink' caused by open sewers in the streets draining into the River Thames and the River Lea.

Part of the solution, devised by Joseph Bazalgette, Chief Engineer of the newly established Metropolitan Board of Works, was the Northern Outfall Sewer. This took sewage from the city's sewer

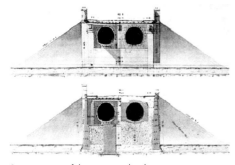

Cross-sections of the sewer embankment where it crossed Abbey Lane

network to a new pumping station at Abbey Mills, at the south-east of the Olympic Park. Work began in 1859 and involved the building of a large embankment carrying two parallel sewer pipes across the valley, passing through the railway embankment.

Many of the bridges built to carry the sewer were recorded as part of the Olympic Park investigations – such as those across the River Lea, Pudding Mill River/Marshgate Lane, Abbey Lane and Channelsea River.

As demand for capacity increased at the start of the 20th century, the embankment was widened and two more pipes added. Differences in the architectural detailing between the first and second phases of construction reflect society's changing perceptions and values.

Northern Outfall Sewer under construction

The original architecture was ornate in its style, demonstrating a civic pride in a pioneering new engineering project. The plainer 20th-century fabric points to a more functional and utilitarian perception of the sewer network.

The sewer survives in the modern landscape as an earthen embankment, along the top of which runs the public footpath and cycleway known as 'The Greenway'.

21

The Clarnico factory

The only industrial building to be preserved within the Olympic Park is the former Starch Department building at the Clarnico confectionery manufacturers. The building will form part of the new Energy Centre.

The Starch Department was one of six buildings recorded in detail at the company's Kings Yard site. Clarnico (short for Clarke, Nickolls & Coombs Ltd) was founded in 1872 at Hackney Wick, and grew rapidly. The Kings Yard buildings were built in the first decade of the 20th century, as the works expanded to span both sides of the Hackney Cut canal.

The other buildings recorded at Kings Yard were the Lozenge Department, Peel Shed, Engine Shed, Coach House (Fire Engine House), and Stables. Together they represent an important survival of an early Edwardian industrial complex.

Left: The Starch Department of the Clarnico confectionery factory on the Hackney Cut canal

Right: Cross-section of the Starch Department building

From the outside, the three-storey Starch Department looks like a traditional 19th-century industrial building, with load-bearing brick walls, and uniform and regularly spaced arched windows on all floors. However, its internal structure, which included an all-steel frame, was 'transitional' in character, demonstrating the shift from 19th to 20th century construction techniques and building materials.

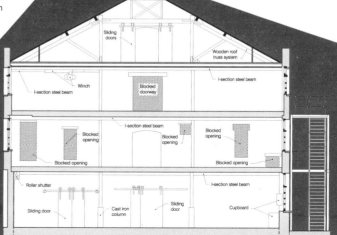

Second World War defences

The wartime defences included a Type-22 concrete pillbox situated beside the Northern Outfall Sewer embankment, on the west side of its bridge across the River Lea. Next to it was a line of four concrete tank blocks strung across the embankment. These guarded what would have been an obvious access route into the city by invading armoured forces.

A Second World War helmet recovered from the site

Left: Aerial view of part of the anti-aircraft battery site

Further north (near the site of the Velodrome) there were defences against attack from the air – an anti-aircraft battery, built just before the war, and a radar station built during it. The anti-aircraft battery had four octagonal gun emplacements, three of which were investigated, along with a magazine, a cordite store with blast walls, a possible Bofor gun emplacement and a command post.

The battery (numbered ZE 21) was sited within the Inner Artillery Zone (AIR 2/4768) and manned by 128th Rocket Anti-Aircraft Battery (101st City of London Home Guard). It was the first battery to shoot down an enemy plane during the inaugural raid of the Blitz on 7 September 1940. A month later the site was hit by a high explosive bomb, and it suffered further damage from VI bombs (doodlebugs) in July and August 1944.

The battery site was converted to a Civil Defence training ground during the 1950s and was decommissioned in 1968, before being partially demolished in 1971.

Oral history

The story of the Olympic Park site was brought up to date at the oral history sessions, where local residents recalled growing up and working in the area.

One interviewee's parents worked for Clarnico confectioners, and Yardley's soap and perfume factory. His mother had started at Clarnico in 1932, aged 15, working in their box factory, while his father had started at 17, making deliveries by horse and cart.

The father's job was kept open for him during the Second World War, after which the family moved into one of Clarnico's cottages on Wallis Road, near the factory. Eight of the houses, in the row of 10, were occupied by employees, the other two being used to store card for the box factory. The cottage had a bathroom upstairs, but an outside toilet – 'in the winter months it was a bloody nightmare!'

The Clarnico fire brigade

The cottages were cheap to rent, but if you lived there it was part of the deal that you had to join Clarnico's fire brigade. When there was a fire at the factory, they would pump water out of the canal.

Employees could eat as many sweets as they liked – but after their first day they would not want any more. However, if you were caught taking sweets home you were 'out the door' – although once a fortnight you could buy two pounds of mis-shapen sweets for sixpence. Sweet rationing ended in 1953.

Inside the Clarnico sweet factory

Workers at the Yardley & Co soap and perfume factory on Carpenter's Road

The wide-ranging nature of the Olympic Park investigations means that there is more than one story to tell about the history of the site. Here we examine a number of themes which recur throughout the evidence found – the river, the evolving landscape, life at home and at work, and the London influence.

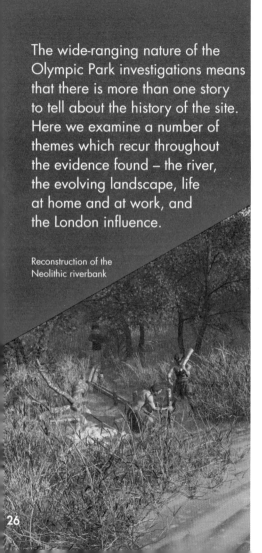

Reconstruction of the Neolithic riverbank

The river

The River Lea is the one constant running through the site's history. Even so, it has constantly changed – in its form, its uses and in the perceptions of the people who lived and worked along it.

The changing river

As the last Ice Age ended, the river became a torrent of water cutting a new course along the valley floor. In time, its banks stabilised and were colonised by woodland, then settled by people. As rising sea levels slowed the water, the river became increasingly affected by the tides. Regular flooding over its banks created a rich marshland pasture across the valley.

As the river was freed from its original course it split into a number of meandering channels, which in time became Channelsea River, Waterworks River, City Mill River,

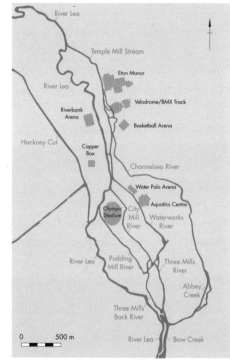

The Victorian waterways

Pudding Mill River, and the River Lea itself. These were straightened and deepened to power the valley's watermills and to aid navigation.

Movement

The river has always been a route through the landscape. For the prehistoric farmers who settled its banks it provided links to more distant communities. As London developed, barges carried produce to its markets from the farmlands of Hertfordshire and beyond.

The barges needed an unobstructed river, but fishers, farmers, millers and water companies also relied on it. So locks were built, the channels scoured and obstructions removed, and eventually completely new navigations, such as the Hackney Cut, were built.

Channelsea River polluted by industry

Perceptions

In prehistory, the placing in the river of precious objects, such as the Neolithic flint axe head, suggests that the river had religious significance. Later, it was a resource to be managed and sustained.

At times, too, the river was feared and reviled – often during floods and when it was used as a sewer, bringing disease and even death. In the end it was neglected, crowded in by dirty industries and polluted by their waste. Channels were abandoned and clogged with rubbish, some were built over and forgotten.

The River Lea renewed

Now there is a new perception of the river's value. The channels were dredged and widened so they could be used to transport materials and waste to and from the site during the construction of the Olympic Park and venues. Wetlands have been established in the north of the Park, creating new sustainable habitats and helping to reduce flood risk.

27

The evolving landscape

As the river changed, so did the landscape it passed through. The physical shape of the valley – the topography and vegetation – have been altered by natural processes and human actions.

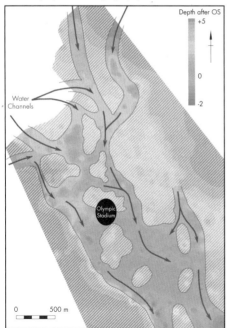

The valley's prehistoric topography

Topography

As the early river cut into the valley floor, it shaped its channels, and created gravel islands and terraces. Stretches of fast- and slow-flowing water, and areas of marsh and dry land, created ecological diversity attractive to prehistoric settlers. However, it was the clearance of woodland and intensive cultivation around the valley that significantly changed the topography. Ploughed soils, washed down by rain, were deposited by river floods as deep sediments across an ever flatter valley floor.

Victorian infrastructure and industry again transformed the topography, with the construction of reservoirs, and of steep embankments for the railway lines and sewer pipes. Finally ground levels were artificially raised to make sites for factories.

The deep excavation site at Temple Mills

In the 20th century, deep dumps of demolition rubble and other waste further disguised the valley's original contours. Now the shape of the landscape has changed again, with the creation of a park with new landforms, widely connected to surrounding areas and with gradients accessible to everyone.

Vegetation

By the time people first arrived in the valley, icy tundra had been replaced by deciduous woodland, with wet grassland and alder carr – woodland marsh – colonising the valley floor. Prehistoric farmers began clearing the woodland on the drier ground, creating areas of open grassland. As flooding

Alder carr woodland

increased, the alder carr receded and a wet but fertile pasture, later improved by drainage, was created on the valley, lasting well into the 19th century.

Human impacts

It is only once prehistoric farmers began to lay out their fields that we see clearly the impact people were starting to have on the landscape. For a long time there were few changes in the way the valley floor was farmed. Some of the ditches surrounding fields, shown on the Ordnance Survey map of 1869, had been first dug in the medieval period.

The medieval causeway across the valley between Bow and Stratford became the focus of long-term settlement, milling and industry. It was primarily to serve these mills that the pattern of waterways was

formalised and maintained. Such changes, however, were dwarfed by those of the 19th century, when the railways and waterworks fragmented the valley. New industries then spread out from Stratford, filling up the accessible land.

Industry, housing, railways and marshland along Waterworks River and Carpenter's Road

Now, remediation works have cleaned up the Olympic Park environment, revitalising the landscape. New parklands, venues and infrastructure have been created within the historical pattern of its river channels.

Life at home and at work

In the study of long-term changes – environmental, archaeological and industrial – it is easy to overlook the individual and daily routines that made up the patterns of people's home and working lives.

Patterns of rural life

It is only in the Bronze Age and Iron Age, when the valley floor was still habitable, that we can first see the houses in which people lived. We can see the timber they worked, and the tools, pottery and other objects they made, traded and used. We find remains of the livestock they tended (cattle, sheep and pigs), the crops they grew (wheat and barley) and the food they ate. From this time, too, we see the ends of their lives – in their cremations and burials.

A medieval plough-team

Their lives become less visible as flooding caused them to move their homes off the valley floor. However, from the Roman period on, we can still see their efforts to manage their landscape – digging ditches, draining the land and improving the water channels.

From the medieval period, documents like the Domesday Book help to fill in some of the gaps, listing the social status of households, the extent of their ploughland, meadow and woodland, their numbers of plough-teams and livestock, and the local watermills and windmills. These mills represent the start of mechanised production.

Reconstruction of the Iron Age round-house and enclosure in Trench 9

Patterns of industrial life

Industry brought new patterns of work. Water power was used not just to grind corn, but also to operate hammers, grinders, saws and bellows. At Temple Mills, people worked in a leather mill, a gunpowder mill (which blew up), bored gun barrels, cut pins, drilled logs for water pipes, printed calico, and made sheet lead, brass kettles and tin plates.

The excavation revealed some of these workers' cottages. Occupants included a cow keeper, silk printer, engineer, sausage-skin maker, domestic servant, butcher, waste paper dealer, factory packer and coffee house keeper, reflecting the increasing diversity of work in the rapidly changing Victorian world.

Inside Great Eastern Railway's Stratford Works

In the early 20th century the area supported an increasingly industrial workforce. The interiors of some of their workplaces were recorded, and details of their working lives in those factories recounted in the oral history sessions.

Selection of domestic finds and tools recovered from the site

0   50 mm

0   50 mm

Children

We also learn of children's lives, so often overlooked by history, such as 13-year-old George Bird and his nine-year-old sister Charlotte, who lived in one of the cottages excavated at Temple Mills. They were at school, but their brother John, aged 15, worked as a wheelwright.

A toy sword was found, along with pieces of a doll's tea-set, marbles, and a painted lead toy figure.

Children's crockery included a mug illustrated with the nursery rhyme 'This is the house that Jack built', while others bore maxims such as 'Creditors have better memories than debtors' by which Victorian parents sought to instil moral values in their children.

Also found were the sometimes doubtful remedies for childhood ailments, like 'Mrs Winslow's Soothing Syrup'. This contained such high levels of alcohol and morphine sulphate that in 1911 it was put on a list of 'baby killers'.

The oral history project captured recollections of childhood. One vivid image is of children scavenging the rubbish dumps near Temple Mills for discarded sweets from the Clarnico confectionery factory.

It was out of a concern for poor east London children that Eton Manor Boys' Club, a sports and social club, was established in Hackney Wick in 1909. Today, the 2012 Games offers new opportunities to inspire children for the enjoyment of both learning and sport.

0   50 mm

Above right: Involving children in the ODA's Discover programme
Above: Selection of children's toys recovered from the site

The London influence

In the last two millennia the site has been increasingly influenced, for better and for worse, by the growth of the nation's capital, and therefore by events on the wider national and international stage.

Routes to and from London

The Roman road across the valley was finally abandoned when it became too dangerous to make the river crossing at Old Ford. Around 1100, Good Queen Maud, wife of Henry I, had a new causeway with bridges built at Stratford-Le-Bow. This influenced the courses of the river channels, the locations of the mills, the areas of settlement, and the spread of industry.

Eight centuries later, the Eastern Counties Railway took a similar line across the valley, carried on a high embankment with numerous bridges over the river channels.

With it came the sprawling goods yards and the Stratford Works, a national centre of railway production and innovation.

The river, too, brought people and goods to London. Wharfs on the riverbank allowed bargemen to avoid the tidal meanders along Bow Creek – and the fees charged at the city's docks on the Thames.

By the 19th century the Hackney Cut and the Limehouse Cut eased navigation to the docklands, providing links to the Empire and the world.

Now, thanks to the London 2012 Games, new transport links have been created to London and beyond, helping with the area's regeneration.

1834 artist's impression of the new railway line being built across the still rural Lea Valley

Industry and economy

Proximity to London's markets offered opportunities for local businesses, from medieval millers to Victorian industrialists. This is reflected in the wide range of manufacturing processes undertaken at Temple Mills.

The valley was also a convenient location for activities that London's citizens could not tolerate.

A 19th-century law banned noxious trades, such as blood, bone and tripe boilers, tallow-melters and fellmongers (sheepskin dealers), from highly populated areas. Many relocated to the former farmland along the Lea, leading to the area's unwelcome nickname of 'Stinky Stratford'.

In fact a varied and vibrant industrial landscape developed, home to engineering works, chemical works,

Tallow melting works on City Mill River, one of Stratford's smelly industries

brick and tile works, confectioners, timber yards, and manufacturers of paints, inks, potted meats, textiles, soaps and perfume, and many more.

War and peace

For many centuries the valley, with its river channels and marshes, was a defensive buffer zone on London's eastern flank. When King Alfred of Wessex made peace with the Viking Guthrum, they agreed a boundary running 'up on the Lea'. This boundary has survived to the present and now marks some of London's boroughs.

Evidence was found for the more recent defence of the capital – including a Second World War anti-aircraft battery near Temple Mills, and a tank block on the Northern Outfall Sewer at Old Ford.

Past, present and future

In 1923, Eton Manor Boys' Club moved to a new site at the north end of the Olympic Park. However, long before London was selected for the 2012 Games, Eton Manor Sports Ground already had a piece of Olympic legacy. Its running track was damaged during the Second World War, and it was replaced with the running track from Wembley Stadium used at the London 1948 Games.

Now the site has become a venue for the 2012 Games. After 2012 it will be transformed into a new sporting facility for both the local community and elite athletes. Remembrance Day monuments commemorating members of the Club who died in the two world wars have been removed for safe-keeping and will be reinstated into the new parklands after the Games.

The long jump at Eton Manor Sports Ground

This is just one instance of how, in its landscape, in its community, and in its rich and varied history, the site of the Olympic Park has been repeatedly renewed. The best of the past has been preserved for the future, and new opportunities – for employment, education, housing, health, sport and recreation, and for wildlife – have been created for future generations.

The investigations have created a new interest in the area's past, raised new questions about the people who lived and worked here, and pointed to a new direction for future archaeological and historical research.